Mini
Sugar Bags

Frances McNaughton

D0525292

Search Press

First published in Great Britain 2013

Search Press Limited
Wellwood, North Farm Road,
Tunbridge Wells, Kent TN2 3DR

Text copyright © Frances McNaughton 2013

Photographs by Paul Bricknell at
Search Press Studios

Photographs and design copyright
© Search Press Ltd 2013

All rights reserved. No part of this book, text,
photographs or illustrations may be reproduced
or transmitted in any form or by any means
by print, photoprint, microfilm, microfiche,
photocopier, internet or in any way known or
as yet unknown, or stored in a retrieval system,
without written permission obtained beforehand
from Search Press.

Print ISBN: 978-1-84448-864-3
Epub ISBN: 978-1-78126-054-8
Mobi ISBN: 978-1-78126-108-8
PDF ISBN: 978-1-78126-162-0

The Publishers and author can accept no
responsibility for any consequences arising from
the information, advice or instructions given in
this publication.

Readers are permitted to reproduce any of the
items in this book for their personal use, or for
the purposes of selling for charity, free of charge
and without the prior permission of the Publishers.
Any use of the items for commercial purposes is
not permitted without the prior permission of
the Publishers.

Suppliers
If you have difficulty in obtaining any of the
materials and equipment mentioned in this book,
then please visit the Search Press website for
details of suppliers: www.searchpress.com

Printed in Malaysia

Dedication

*To my lovely friend Jo (Poppett) who introduced me to
the world of beautiful bags. The pink rose bag
is just for her!*

Contents

Introduction

Following the publication of my book *Mini Sugar Shoes*, it seemed a natural progression to follow with a book of tiny sugar bags. I have again tried to keep the designs and instructions as simple as possible, using basic shapes. I have mostly used a sugar modelling paste known as Mexican paste, which dries slowly and stays easy to handle as it feels leathery before it completely dries. This means that it is much less likely to crack or break during handling, yet it is strong enough to support its own weight when making these small objects. There is a recipe for Mexican paste on page 6.

It is also possible to make these bags using flower paste and other types of modelling paste – try with your own favourite. Edible wafer paper and leaf (sheet) gelatine have been used for different effects to make a couple of the bags. Many of the designs can be adapted to different sizes and colours very easily. They could also be made in non-edible media such as polymer clay or air-drying modelling clay to make them longer lasting.

I hope that by giving you these simple ideas you will have fun creating them, and perhaps develop some of your own using these as an inspiration with different embossers, colours or cutters. Enjoy!

Materials and tools

Materials

Edible wafer paper

Leaf gelatine sheets

Edible gold and silver paint

Tiny edible decorations – sugar balls and edible stars

Edible food colour felt-tip pen

Clear piping gel (to glue and gloss)

White and coloured Mexican paste/ flower paste

Sugarpaste

Tiny white sugar balls

Edible glitter

Edible powder food colour and alcohol

Mexican paste is a sugar modelling paste made with gum, which makes it stronger and allows it to be rolled out thinly. It dries slowly, going leathery before it dries hard. It is available commercially or can be made using the following recipe.

Mexican paste recipe

Place 225g (8oz) icing sugar into a bowl. Add three 5ml teaspoons of gum tragacanth. Mix the dry ingredients together. Add six 5ml teaspoons of cold water. Stir by hand until it becomes crumbly but damp enough to bind together. Add a little more water if too dry, or icing sugar if too wet. Turn out on to a worktop and knead until pliable. Place in a plastic food bag and leave at room temperature for twelve hours until firm.

Break off a small piece and knead between your palms. Continue kneading between your fingers. Repeat until all the paste is softened. The paste can be used straight away.

Store paste in an airtight container at room temperature, never in the fridge. If you have leftover paste, wrap each piece in cling film and place all of the pieces into a plastic food bag and place them in the freezer. Defrost only the quantity required for using. Smaller pieces will defrost more quickly.

Note: Mexican paste and flower paste can also be coloured by adding strong paste food colours. When making dark colours, the paste can become very soft, which is why I like to use ready-coloured black, red and purple paste.

Tools

From bottom left:

Small sharp pointed scissors For trimming ends of paste.

Music stave cutter For cutting thin strips

Small non-stick rolling pin This is used for rolling out the paste.

Dresden tool This is used for marking holes, shaping paste and pressing on fluff or wool without flattening it.

Petal veiner tool For frilling. The scoop end is great for sprinkling glitter.

Tweezers Used to pick up stars for the Starry Evening Bag (page 18).

Large stitching wheel For adding large stitch patterns.

Fine stitching wheel For adding small stitch patterns.

Cutting wheel This is used for cutting shapes from rolled paste.

Fine paintbrush/waterbrush Used for dampening the paste before attaching pieces.

Ruler For measuring and for impressing straight lines into paste.

Small fine palette knife This is used for releasing paste from the work surface and for cutting and marking lines.

Tea strainer/sieve Used to create fluff by pushing sugarpaste through the mesh.

Tiny blossom cutter and oval, circle and square cutters

Garrett frill cutter Used to cut a frilled circle.

Daisy embosser for the Clutch Bag (page 8) and the Sporran (page 46).

Small basketweave embosser for the Basket on page 16.

You will also need a **dusting brush** for applying edible powder food colour (I use a small blusher brush), **plastic sandwich bags** for keeping pieces soft and a **cocktail stitck** and **piping tube** for marking holes.

Clutch Bag

Materials:
Black Mexican paste/flower paste
Edible gold powder food colour

Tools:
Small, non-stick rolling pin
2.5cm (1in) square cutter
3.5cm (1⅜in) fluted oval cutter
Small daisy embosser
Fine stitching wheel
Dusting brush

Instructions:
1 Roll the paste thinly. Cut out one square and one fluted oval.

2 Fold the square in half. Run the stitching wheel along the two sides.

3 Use the square cutter to cut into the fluted oval as shown. Emboss with a small daisy embosser.

4 Brush edible gold powder lightly over the fluted piece. Dampen the back and attach over the top of the folded bag.

Opposite
Sweet Sophistication
Make this sugar beauty for someone who loves simple yet sophisticated style. For an alternative look, make the clutch bag in white and dust pink and green powder on the flower.

Purple Banana Bag

Materials:

Purple Mexican paste/flower paste

Tools:

Small, non-stick rolling pin

6cm (2³⁄₈in) and 2.5cm (1in) circle cutters

2cm (¾in) and 1cm (³⁄₈in) oval cutters

Fine stitching wheel

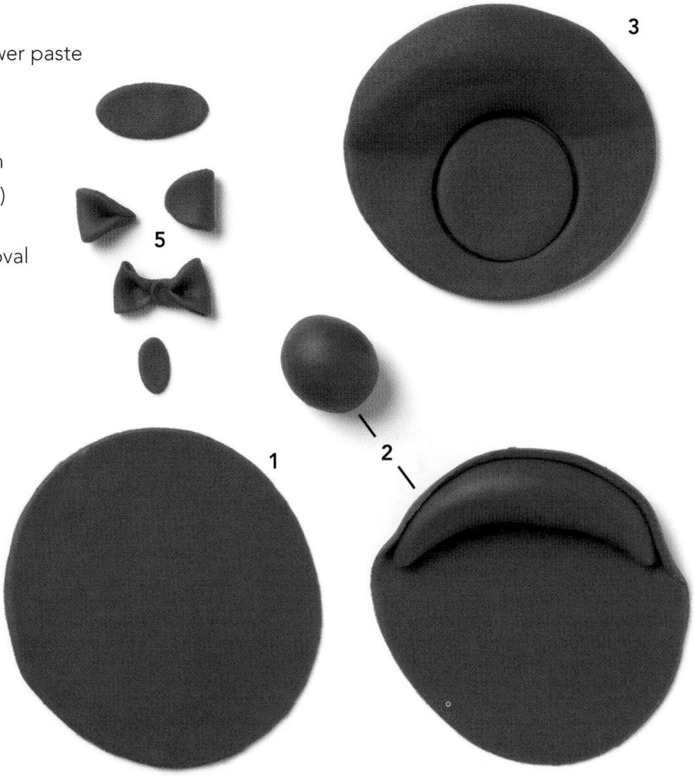

Instructions:

1 Roll out the paste thinly. Cut out two 6cm (2³⁄₈in) circles, two 2cm (¾in) ovals and one 1cm (³⁄₈in) oval.

2 Shape a large pea-sized piece of paste into a 6cm (2³⁄₈in) banana shape. Attach it just inside the edge of one of the 6cm (2³⁄₈in) circles. Dampen the edge of the circle and stick it to the banana part.

3 Attach the second circle on top of the first one, curving and smoothing the edge over the bottom to hide the join. Use the 2.5cm (1in) circle cutter to cut the hole for the handle.

4 Mark the bag with the stitching wheel as shown.

5 For the bow, fold the two 2cm (¾in) ovals in half and pinch the narrow ends. Dampen and press the ends together and lay the 1cm (³⁄₈in) oval across the join, tucking the ends under.

6 Dampen the bow and attach it to the bag.

Red Glitter Bag

Materials:

Red Mexican paste/flower paste
Edible red glitter
Piping gel

Tools:

Small, non-stick rolling pin
4cm (1½in) square cutter
0.5cm (¼in) oval cutter
Music stave cutter
Fine stitching wheel
Fine paintbrush

Instructions:

1 Roll the paste 3mm (⅛in)thick. Cut out two 0.5cm (¼in) ovals. Leave to dry.

2 Roll the paste thinly. Cut one 4cm (1½in) square and one strip using the music stave cutter.

3 Dampen along two sides of the square. Stand the ovals up on their ends about halfway down the sides of the square. Bring the bottom flap up over the edges of the ovals and then bring the top flap over to overlap the bottom flap.

4 Mark along the strip with the fine stitching wheel. Attach the ends to the sides of the bag.

5 For best results, allow the surface of the bag to dry before sticking the glitter on. Lay the bag on a piece of paper or plastic, so that the excess glitter can be poured back into the jar. Spread a thin layer of piping gel on the top flap of the bag. Sprinkle the edible glitter on to it. Use a dry paintbrush to brush away the excess glitter.

Glamour Girl

Make an alternative bag in pure white with white sparkles. These bags would look perfect on a cake for someone with an eye for glamorous accessories.

Shopping Bag

Materials:

Edible wafer paper
Edible food colour felt-tip pen
Piping gel

Tools:

Small, sharp pointed scissors
Ruler
Fine paintbrush
Dresden tool

Instructions:

1 Cut wafer paper with scissors:

- Two pieces 4 x 5cm (1½ x 2in) for the front and back
- Two pieces 5 x 1.5cm (2 x ⅝in) for the sides
- One piece 4 x 1.5cm (1½ x ⅝in) for the base
- Two pieces 4 x 2mm (1½ x ¹⁄₁₆in) for the handles.

2 Draw your chosen design on the front panel using an edible food colour felt-tip pen.

3 Brush the ends of the handles with a little piping gel. Attach one each to the inside of the front and back panels as shown. Press the ends of the handles firmly to the panels using the flat part of the Dresden tool to make sure they stick.

4 Brush the side and bottom edges of the back and front panel with piping gel. Attach the side and bottom panels to the back panel.

5 Finally lay the front panel gently on top. Carefully stand the bag up.

Shopaholic's Delight

These bags make the perfect cake topper for someone who loves shopping. Decorate the bags in the style of their favourite shops. White wafer paper can also be coloured all over by brushing with edible powder food colours.

Basket

Materials:

Beige Mexican paste/
  flower paste

Tools:

Small, non-stick rolling pin

4cm (1½in) square cutter

Ruler

Cutting wheel

3cm (1¼in) oval cutter

Small basketweave embosser

Cocktail stick

Instructions:

1 Roll the paste out
to 3mm (⅛in). Cut an
oblong 1.5 x 4cm (⅝
x 1½in). Allow to dry
until it feels leathery.

2 Roll the paste thinly. Cut out two 3cm (1⅛in) ovals. Cut one end off each oval using the
cutting wheel to make a 2cm (¾in) high arch for the sides. Emboss the surface with the
small basketweave embosser. Roll the paste thinly again. Emboss the surface with the small
basketweave embosser as before. Cut out one 4cm (1½in) square and one 4 x 2cm
(1½ x ¾in) oblong.

3 Dampen the edges of the base and attach the arched sides. Stick the small basketweave
oblong to the base and sides, and the square to the base and sides, overlapping the oblong
to make the front of the basket. Make two holes for the handles with a cocktail stick.

4 Make two very thin sausages of paste. Twist them together to make the handle. Cut the
length to 4cm (1½in). Dampen the holes and attach the handles.

5 Make a tiny loop from a thin sausage of the paste. Stick on the front of the basket on the
edge of the overlap.

Starry Evening Bag

Materials:

Purple and white Mexican paste/
   flower paste
Tiny edible gold stars
Tiny gold-coloured sugar balls
Edible gold paint
Piping gel

Tools:

Small, non-stick rolling pin
6cm (2³⁄₈in) circle cutter
Cutting wheel
Ruler
Tweezers
Fine paintbrush

Instructions:

1 Roll the purple paste thinly. Cut out the 6cm (2³⁄₈in) circle.
Pinch small gathers around the edge.

2 Bring all the pinched edges together and press them
gently until the gathers form a 2.5cm (1in) edge. Press
the edge on to the surface and use the rolling pin to
flatten the gathered edge. Cut straight across with
the cutting wheel. Stand the bag up.

3 Roll out the white paste thinly. Cut a strip 2.5 x
1cm (1 x ³⁄₈in). Press a line down the centre without
cutting through. Fold along the line. Dampen the
straight cut edge of the purple gathered bag and
stick the folded white oblong over the top.

4 Paint the folded part with edible gold paint and a
fine paintbrush.

5 Attach the tiny edible stars by picking up each star
with tweezers and touching the star on piping gel before
placing on the surface of the bag.

6 Stick two tiny gold-coloured sugar balls to the top of the
bag with a little piping gel.

Black Patent Bag

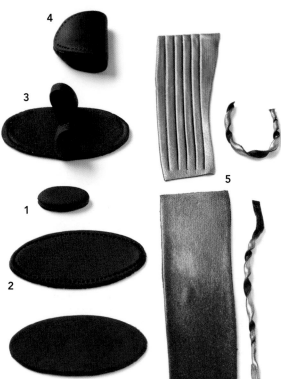

Materials:

Black Mexican paste/flower paste

Gold edible powder food colour

Tiny gold sugar pearls

4mm (³/₁₆in) edible black
    sugar pearls

Piping gel

Tools:

Small non-stick rolling pin

5cm (2in) and 2cm (¾in)
    oval cutters

Music stave cutter

Dresden tool

Fine stitching wheel

Dusting brush

Small sharp pointed
    scissors

Fine paintbrush

Instructions:

1 For the sides, roll out the paste
to the thickness of 2–3mm (¹/₈in).
Cut two ovals using the 2cm (¾in)
cutter. Allow the paste to dry for a few minutes, turning it
over occasionally.

2 Roll out the paste thinly. Allow to dry slightly on each side until it feels
leathery. Cut out the 5cm (2in) oval. Run the fine stitching wheel round the edge.

3 Turn the oval over. Dampen around the edges of the smaller ovals (the sides).
Attach them standing, as shown, in the middle on the edge of the 5cm (2in) oval.

4 Bring the oval together using the smaller ovals as supports for the sides of
the bag. Join together at the top or overlap the top edge.

5 Roll out the paste very thinly. Allow to dry slightly on each side until
the paste feels leathery. Brush gold edible powder colour on one side
of the paste. Cut the strap using the music stave cutter. Brush over
just one side of the side firmly with the gold powder. Twist one of the
straps so that the black and gold both show. Dampen both sides of
the bag. Attach one end of the strap to the side of the bag. Cut the
other end to your chosen length and attach it to the other side of the
bag. If you want the strap to stand, leave the bag lying down until the
strap has dried.

6 Spread clear piping gel over the body and sides of the bag using the paintbrush to make it shine. Attach a gold sugar pearl at each end of the strap, and the black sugar pearls across the top join. The piping gel will hold the sugar pearls in place. Handle the bag carefully as the strap will be fragile, and the bag will stay tacky.

Pink Rose Bag

Materials:

Bright pink Mexican paste/
flower paste

Pearl white edible powder
food colour

and water

A little alcohol for painting

Tools:

Small, non-stick rolling pin

Garrett frill cutter

Petal veiner tool

6cm (2³⁄₈in) and 2.5cm (1in)
circle cutters

Dresden tool

No. 2 or 3 piping tube

Cocktail stick

Cutting wheel/ sharp knife

Music stave cutter

Large stitching wheel

Small sharp pointed scissors

Waterbrush/fine paintbrush

Plastic sandwich bag

Instructions:

1 Roll out the paste thinly. Allow it to dry slightly on each side until it feels leathery.
Cut out a frilled circle with the Garrett frill cutter, the straps using the music stave
cutter, one 2.5cm (1in) circle, a strip of paste 1 x 8.5cm (³⁄₈ x 3³⁄₈in), and a very tiny
thin strip for the stay on the strap.

2 Cut the middle out of the frilled circle using the 6cm (2³⁄₈in) circle. Cover the other pieces with the plastic sandwich bag to keep soft
until required.

3 Further frill around the Garrett frill by rolling the edge firmly
with the petal veiner tool.

4 Dampen around the inside (flat edge) and fold the frill on
to itself to make a double layer frill. Dampen along the flat
edge of the double frill and carefully roll up to make a rose.

5 Curve the petals outwards and tweak to make a rose
shape. Make sure that the edges of the petals will make the
rose slightly bigger than the 2.5cm (1in) base of the bag.

6 Roll the large stitching wheel down the middle of the wider strip of paste twice to make a stitching pattern to look like a zip. Paint the zip with pearl white edible powder mixed with a little alcohol, using the fine paintbrush.

7 Turn the strip over; dampen along one long side edge. Wrap it around the 2.5cm (1in) circle. Dampen where the strip overlaps to join it.

8 Mark two of the music stave cutter strips with a piping tube at one end. Attach one of the straps to the circle bag. Cut the remaining strap to a point at the other end and mark tiny holes with a cocktail stick. Attach the strap to the bag. Join the straps by overlapping. Attach the tiny thin strip around the straps. Paint that thin strip and the two tiny circle marks with the pearl white edible powder mixed with a little alcohol.

9 Dampen the centre of the bag and attach the rose in the centre.

Zebra Print Bag

Materials:

White and black Mexican
paste/flower paste

4mm (³/₁₆in) edible black sugar
pearls

Piping gel

Tools:

Small, non-stick rolling pin

3cm (1¼in) oval cutter

6cm (2³/₈in) circle cutter

No. 2 or 3 piping tube

Small, fine palette knife

Cutting wheel

Dresden tool

Small sharp pointed scissors

Waterbrush/fine paintbrush
and water

Instructions:

1 Roll out the white paste to around 3mm (¹/₈in) thick. Cut out the 3cm (1¼in) oval.

2 Roll out the white paste thinly. Mark with the 6cm (2³/₈in) circle without cutting through. Use scissors to make lots of tiny black pointed pieces of paste as shown. Lay them over the white paste to form a zebra pattern and roll over with a rolling pin to fuse the colours together.

3 Cut the 6cm (2³/₈in) circle. Use the cutting wheel to cut the circle in half, and cut a small piece 0.5cm off each end as shown. Use the piping tube to mark two holes in each side of the bag where the handles will be attached.

4 Dampen around the oval base and the inside, curved edge of the bag sides. Attach one side to the oval base, and then attach the other side to the first side, making sure that they line up.

5 To make the rope handles, roll pieces of white and black paste each to make a very thin sausage about 12cm (4¾in) long. Twirl the two colour pieces together, rolling to form a spiral. Cut to make two handles about 6cm (2³/₈in) long. Dampen the inside marks on the bag and attach the handles.

6 Place a tiny dot of piping gel on the outer side where the handles join, and stick a black sugar pearl in place. Repeat at all the handle joining points. Prop the bag up to dry.

Leopard Vanity Case

Materials:

Black and beige Mexican paste/ flower paste

Black and autumn leaf food colouring

Tools:

Small, non-stick rolling pin

3cm (1¼in) oval cutter

Music stave cutter

Small fine palette knife

Cutting wheel

Ruler

Dresden tool

Large stitching wheel

Tissue or cotton wool

Small, sharp pointed scissors

Waterbrush/fine paintbrush and water

Small fine paintbrush for painting

Plastic sandwich bag

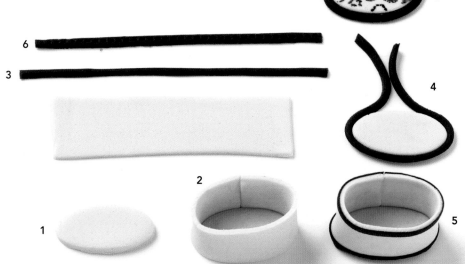

Instructions:

1 For the base and lid, roll out the beige paste to around 2mm (¹⁄₁₆in). Cut out two 3cm (1¼in) ovals. Leave to dry for a few minutes, until they feel leathery.

2 Roll out the beige paste thinly. Allow to dry slightly on each side until the paste feels leathery. Cut a strip 2 x 7.5cm (¾ x 3in) using the cutting wheel. Dampen the sides of the oval base and wrap the strip around to make the sides stand up. Dampen to join the ends and press the seams with the Dresden tool. Prop up with a little tissue or cotton wool until the piece holds its shape.

3 Roll out the black paste thinly. Allow to dry slightly on each side until the paste feels leathery. Cut out three small strips using the music stave cutter. Keep them covered under a plastic sandwich bag to keep them soft until ready to use.

4 Dampen around the edge of the oval lid and attach one of the strips. Cut off the excess.

5 Attach black strips at the base and top of the upright sides of the bag as shown.

6 Run the stitching wheel along another black strip and carefully attach it around on top of the top edge of the sides to look like a zip.

7 Paint tiny splodgy circles of dark brown or black food colouring all over the beige parts, and then fill inside the outlines by painting with autumn leaf colour.

8 Attach another black strip for the handle on the top of the lid. Use a strip slightly longer than the lid and stick it on at each end, leaving the middle raised. When the parts are dry enough to hold their shape, attach the lid to the sides.

Gel Bag

Materials:

Yellow Mexican paste/flower paste
Leaf gelatine sheets
Piping gel

Tools:

Small, non-stick rolling pin
Cutting wheel
Ruler
4cm (1½in) and 1cm (³⁄₈in) oval cutters
Tiny blossom cutter
Small, sharp pointed scissors

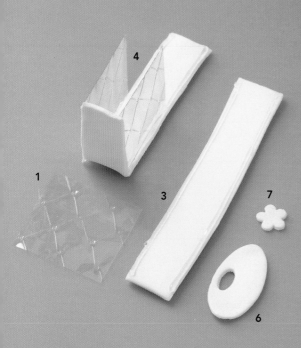

Instructions:

1 Cut the gelatine sheets to make two 4cm (1½in) squares using the scissors.

2 Roll the yellow paste thinly. Leave to dry for a few minutes on each side until it feels leathery.

3 Use the cutting wheel to cut a strip 2 x 13cm (¾ x 5¹⁄₈in) from the paste.

4 Pipe a thin line of piping gel along both long sides, slightly in from the edge. Start at one end of the strip and press both squares of gelatine gently into the paste. Roll the gelatine along the strip, pressing into the paste each time.

5 When the paste surrounds three sides of the gelatine, cut off the excess paste in line with the gelatine square.

6 Roll out the paste thinly. Allow to dry for a few minutes on each side. Cut out two 4cm (1½in) ovals. Cut the hole for the handle towards one side of each oval using the 1cm (³⁄₈in) oval cutter.

7 Cut out two of the blossoms.

8 Spread a little piping gel on the back of each oval and press into place at the top of the bag to form the handle.

9 Attach a blossom to each gelatine side of the bag with a little piping gel.

Make an alternative in red. These bright bags look perfect for the beach or summer shopping.

Sheepskin Bag

Materials:

Mexican paste/flower paste coloured with autumn leaf/cream food colouring

Sugarpaste coloured slightly paler than the Mexican paste

Tools:

Small, non-stick rolling pin

6cm (2³⁄₈in) square cutter

Ruler

Fine stitching wheel

No. 2 or 3 piping tube

Small sieve/tea strainer

Cocktail stick

Small sharp pointed scissors

Instructions:

1 Roll out the Mexican paste thinly. Leave to dry for a few minutes on each side until it feels leathery. Cut out one 6cm (2³⁄₈in) square.

2 Mark two lines for the base by pressing the ruler into the paste 2.75cm (1¹⁄₁₆in) from each end. Be careful not to cut through. Fold along each line and bring the sides together, dampening if necessary.

3 Run a stitching wheel along both sides and across the ends of the base

4 Stand the bag up for a few minutes, propping it up with cotton wool until it holds its shape.

5 Make the fur trim by pressing small amounts of the pale cream sugarpaste through a small sieve or tea strainer. Cut the fluff off and cut it into small strips using scissors.

6 Dampen the sides and top edge of the bag and attach the fur, pressing into place with a cocktail stick without flattening the fur.

7 Roll a very thin sausage of Mexican paste and cut two 6cm (2³⁄₈in) lengths for the handles. Push in the piping tube at each end to make a stud.

8 Dampen the ends of the handles and press into place. Prop up the bag and handles with cotton wool until they hold their shape.

Purple Square Bag

Materials:

Purple Mexican paste/flower paste
Beige Mexican paste/flower paste
Tiny gold-coloured sugar balls
Piping gel

Tools:

Small, non-stick rolling pin
1.5cm square cutter
1cm (³/₈in) and 0.5cm
　(¹/₈in) circle cutters
Cutting wheel
Fine stitching wheel
Ruler
Music stave cutter
Cocktail stick
Plastic sandwich bag

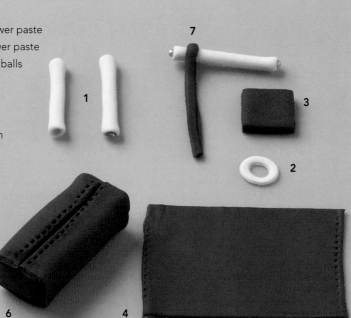

Instructions:

1 Roll a very thin sausage of beige Mexican paste and cut two 3cm (1¼in) lengths for the handles. Make a small dip in each end using a cocktail stick. Attach a tiny gold sugar ball at each end with a little piping gel. Leave to dry.

2 Roll out the beige Mexican paste thinly and cut out four 1cm (³/₈in) circles. Cut the middles of each circle out with the 0.5cm (¹/₈in) circle. Leave to dry for a few minutes.

3 Roll out the purple Mexican paste thinly. Cut out two 1.5cm squares and leave to dry for a few minutes.

4 Roll out the purple Mexican paste thinly. Allow to dry on both sides until it feels leathery. Cut an oblong 6 x 4cm (2³/₈ x 1½in). Run the fine stitching wheel along both short ends – this will later form the zip.

5 Cut the straps from the thin paste using the music stave cutter. Keep covered with a plastic sandwich bag until ready to use.

6 Dampen the sides of the oblong and stand the two squares half way along each long side. Bring the sides of the oblong over the squares to form the bag, butting the top together to look like a zip.

7 Dampen the two thin purple straps and place the handle in the middle of each strap. Stick the straps to themselves over the handle.

8 Thread a circle up each strap.

9 Dampen the sides and under the bag where the straps will go. Attach the straps to the bag, so they stand up straight, then cut off the excess under the bag.

10 Attach two tiny gold sugar balls for the end of the zip with piping gel.

11 Lay the bag on its side to dry.

Camouflage Bag

Materials:

Green, grey-brown, brown, autumn leaf and black Mexican paste/ flower paste

Tools:

Small, non-stick rolling pin

Cutting wheel

Fine stitching wheel

Ruler

Music stave cutter

2cm (¾in) square cutter

Cocktail stick

Plastic sandwich bag

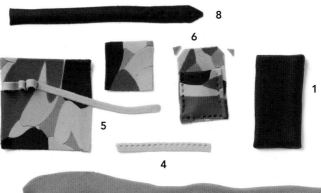

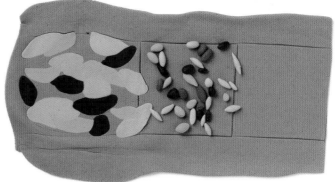

Instructions:

1 Roll out black Mexican paste to 3mm (⅛in). Cut out an oblong 4 x 2cm (1½ x ¾in). Allow to dry for a few minutes until it feels leathery.

2 Make twenty to thirty small rice-size pieces each of green, brown, autumn leaf and black paste. Keep them covered under a plastic sandwich bag so they stay soft.

3 Roll out the grey-brown paste thinly. Mark a long oblong approximately 16 x 4cm (6¼ x 1½in) with the cutting wheel but without cutting through. Scatter the coloured pieces of paste over the surface. Press in gently with your fingers to make sure they stick, then roll over the surface with a rolling pin to form a camouflage pattern. Cut the paste to form the large oblong. Cut that oblong to make two 4cm (1½in) squares, two 3 x 2cm (1¼ x ¾in) pieces and four 2cm (¾in) squares. Keep covered under a plastic sandwich bag to stay soft.

4 Roll the green paste thinly. Allow to dry for a few minutes until it feels leathery. Cut out thin strips using the music stave cutter. Cut three of them to 4cm (1½in). Run the fine stitching wheel along the edges of two of them to form the zip. The third one is to make the loops on the side of the bag.

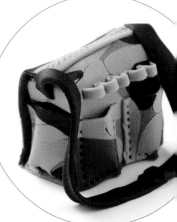

5 Dampen a line along one of the 4cm (1½in) squares 1cm (³/₈in) in from the edge. Attach one end of a long green strip, holding the other end up. Lay a cocktail stick on the surface and press the strip over it, forming a loop. Continue forming loops and sticking on the strip.

6 For the pockets, use the fine stitching wheel to stitch around three edges of each of the 2cm (¾in) squares. Stick two pockets on to the square with the looped green strip; and one pocket each on the 3 x 2cm (1¼ x ¾in) sides. Cut the top corners off the two sides.

7 Dampen the edges of the thick black base. Attach the sides to the base. Dampen three edges of the 4cm squares. Stick them to the base and sides of the bag with the pockets at the bottom. Dampen the stitched green strips and stick them in place on the top of the bag.

8 Roll out black paste thinly. Cut two 1 x 6cm straps (³/₈ x 2³/₈in) and one very thin strip 1.5cm x 2mm (½ x ¹/₈in). Cut the end of one of the long straps to a point and make holes with a cocktail stick. Stick the pointed end overlapping the other strap. Stick the tiny strip around where the straps overlap. Dampen the sides of the bag and attach the straps.

Backpack

Materials:

Beige Mexican paste/
flower paste

Tools:

Small, non-stick rolling pin

4cm (1½in), 3cm (1¼in) and
2cm (¾in) oval cutters

4cm (1½in) and 1cm (³⁄₈in)
square cutters

Fine stitching wheel

Cutting wheel

Music stave cutter

Plastic sandwich bag

Cocktail stick

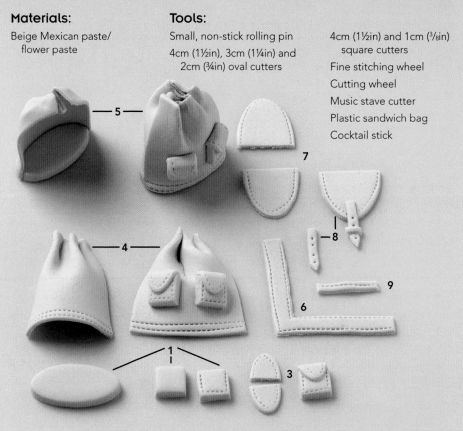

Instructions:

1 Roll the paste 3mm (¹⁄₈in) thick. Cut out the 3cm (1¼in) oval for the base and two 1cm (³⁄₈in) squares for the pockets. Run the fine stitching wheel round three edges of the pockets.

2 Roll the paste out thinly. Cut out three 4cm (1½in) squares, one 2cm (¾in) oval, one 4cm (1½in) oval and one thin strip using the music stave cutter. Keep all under a plastic bag to stay soft.

3 Cut the 2cm (¾in) oval in half and mark around the edge with the fine stitching wheel. Dampen the backs and stick over the top edges of the pockets.

4 Mark a double stitching line along one edge of two of the 4cm squares. Attach the pockets to one of the squares. Gather the top edge of the squares together, forming little folds.

5 Dampen around the oval base and attach the first square, then the one with the pockets. Stick the two sides to each other with a little water.

6 Cut the third 4cm (1½in) square to a 'v' shape by cutting again with the 4cm (1½in) square cutter. Mark along the edges with the stitching wheel. Attach the 'v' to the top part of the back of the bag. Stick the ends lower down the bag to form the back straps, with the stitching showing.

7 To make the top flap, cut the 4cm (1½in) oval in half and mark round the edge of one half with the stitching wheel.

8 Cut one of the thin straps to 1.5cm (⅝in). Cut one end to a point. Mark holes with a cocktail stick. Cut a very thin strip and attach around the end of the strap. Stick the strap on to the half oval. Dampen the back of the half oval and stick over the top of the bag.

9 Mark another thin strip with the stitching wheel. Cut to 2cm (¾in). Dampen each end and attach to the top of the flap.

Denim Bag

Materials:

Beige and blue Mexican paste/flower paste

Yellow and white food colouring (powder or paste) and food grade alcohol or water

Tiny gold-coloured sugar balls

Piping gel

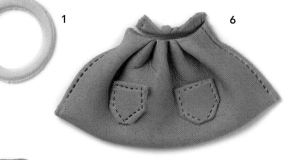

Tools:

Small, non-stick rolling pin

6cm (2³⁄₈in) and 1cm (³⁄₈in) square cutters

2cm (¾in) and 1.5cm (⁵⁄₈in) circle cutters

Cutting wheel

Fine stitching wheel

Fine paintbrush

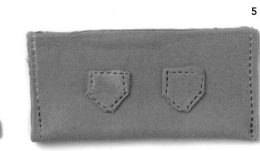

Instructions:

1 To make the handles, roll out the beige paste thinly. Cut out two 2cm (¾in) circles and cut the centres out with the 1.5cm (⁵⁄₈in) circle cutter. Allow to dry until the handles hold their shape.

2 Roll out the blue paste thinly. Cut out one 6cm (2³⁄₈in) square and two 1cm (³⁄₈in) squares.

3 Fold the large square in half and run the fine stitching wheel down the sides to join them.

4 Cut two corners from each of the smaller squares. Mark around the edges with the stitching wheel to make pockets. Stick the pockets on to one side of the bag.

5 Mix white food colouring with a few drops of alcohol or water. Add a small amount of yellow food colouring. The white colouring will make the yellow show up on the blue paste. Paint along the lines of stitching down the sides and on the pockets.

6 Carefully gather the top of the bag together with little folds. Press gently then cut through the top with the 2cm (¾in) circle cutter.

7 Dampen the curved cut edge and attach the handles.

8 Attach tiny gold sugar balls on the corners of the bag and pockets using small dots of piping gel.

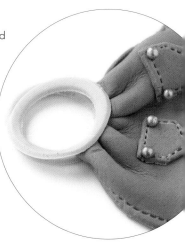

Designer Satchel

Materials:

Mexican paste/flower paste coloured with dark brown and autumn leaf food colouring

Edible gold paint

Tools:

Small, non-stick rolling pin

5cm (2in) oval cutter

Music stave cutter

Cutting wheel

Ruler

Fine paintbrush

Cocktail stick

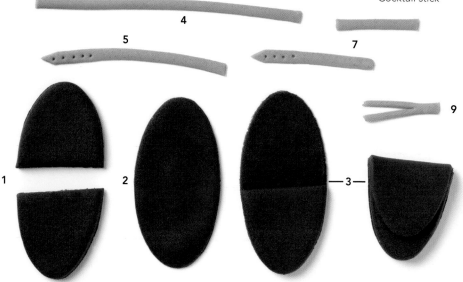

Instructions:

1 Roll the dark brown paste to 3mm (⅛in) thick. Cut out the 5cm (2in) oval. Cut in half.

2 Roll the dark brown paste thinly. Cut another 5cm (2in) oval.

3 Dampen the thin oval. Stick the thick half-oval on top then fold the rest of the thin oval over the front to create the bag.

4 Roll the autumn leaf paste thinly. Cut thin strips using the music stave cutter. Cut two strips to 7cm (2¾in). Attach one of the straps to the side of the bag.

5 Cut the end of the other strap to a point. Mark holes with a cocktail stick.

6 Stick the pointed end to the other strap and attach the other end to the bag.

7 Attach a short strap at the bottom of the bag and cut off the excess. Take another strap, cut the end to a point and mark holes with a cocktail stick.

8 Attach the pointed strap over the top of the bag, overlapping the bottom strap.

9 Cut some of the remaining bits of strip in half to make very thin strips. You need three.

10 Attach two very thin strips on the vertical bag strap and one around the handle strap.

11 Paint one on the bag and the other on the handle with edible gold paint to look like buckles. Indent the one on the bag with a cocktail stick.

Red Lips

Materials:

Red Mexican paste/flower paste
Edible silver paint
Tiny silver-coloured sugar balls
Piping gel

Tools:

Small, non-stick rolling pin
Dresden tool
Cutting wheel
Large stitching
 wheel
Fine paintbrush
Ruler

2

4

1

Instructions:

1 Roll two sausages of paste approximately 6cm x 5mm (2³⁄₈ x ¼in).

2 Pinch the ends together. Make the top lip shape by pushing in the middle with a Dresden tool.

3 Roll the paste thinly. Allow to dry slightly on the surface.

4 Lay the lip shape on top of the paste. Cut closely around the shape for one piece and about 1cm (³⁄₈in) larger for the second.

5 Attach the lip shape on top of the smaller mouth.

6 Use the large stitching wheel to mark two stitching lines along the middle of the larger mouth shape. If the mouth is to be unzipped, cut between the stitching lines.

7 Dampen the back of the paste and lay it over the lip shape. Shape the paste over and pinch the pointed ends. Mark gentle creases in the lips with the Dresden tool.

8 Brush over the surface with piping gel and a fine paintbrush. Attach silver-coloured sugar balls at one end of the zip.

9 Paint the zip with edible silver paint and a fine paintbrush. Handle the bag carefully as it will stay tacky.

Hot Lips

These lippy sugar bags can be made with the lips open or tightly zipped. Make them to adorn a cake for a bag lover with a sense of humour as well as a sense of style.

Hearts and Flowers

Materials:

White Mexican paste/
   flower paste

White pearl edible powder
   food colour

Tiny white sugar balls

Piping gel

Tools:

Small, non-stick rolling pin

2cm (¾in) heart cutter

2cm (¾in) and 1cm (⅜in) oval
   cutters

Cutting wheel

Tiny blossom cutter

Dusting brush

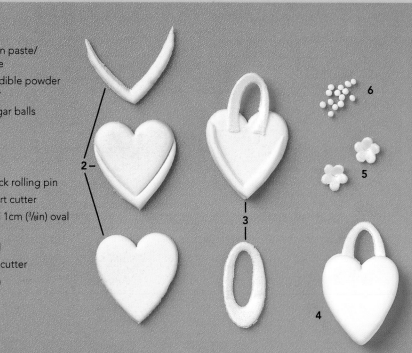

Instructions:

1 Roll the paste thickly to around 2mm (¹/₁₆in). Cut out three hearts. Allow to dry until they feel leathery.

2 Use the heart cutter to cut one of the hearts again to form a 'v' shape. Stick this 'v' on top of another of the hearts. This forms the back piece of the heart bag.

3 Roll the paste thinly. Brush over the surface with edible white pearl powder. Cut out a 2cm (¾in) oval for the handle. Cut the middle out with the 1cm (⅜in) oval. Cut off one end of the oval. Stick the handle on to the back piece.

4 Attach the other heart on top of the back piece.

5 Dampen the surface of the bag. Cut out tiny blossoms. You can use the plunger to push the blossoms into position.

6 Brush a thin line of piping gel on to the handle. Sprinkle with the tiny white sugar balls. If you want the handle to look neater, remove the excess white sugar balls, then the piping gel will allow time to rearrange them neatly.

Sporran

Materials:

Black and white Mexican
  paste/flower paste
White sugarpaste
Edible silver sugar balls
Edible silver paint
Piping gel

Tools:

Small, non-stick rolling pin
2.5cm (1in) and 2cm (¾in) circle
  cutters
1cm (³⁄₈in) square cutter
Cutting wheel
Large stitching wheel

Garrett frill cutter/ large fluted
  cutter
Small daisy embosser
Small sieve/tea strainer
Small fine palette knife
Cocktail stick

Instructions:

1 Roll out the black paste to 2mm (¹⁄₈in) thick. Cut out one 2.5cm (1in) circle and one 2cm (¾in) circle.

2 Gently narrow one end of the larger circle. Mark three lines with the large stitching wheel to represent chains.

3 Cut across the smaller circle with the Garrett frill cutter to make the two curves. Press with the embosser. Paint with edible silver paint.

46

4 Paint the stitch lines lightly with edible silver paint. Make the fur trim by pressing small amounts of white sugarpaste through a small sieve/tea strainer. Use the palette knife to cut the fur off from the other side, and cut it into small strips. Dampen the edges of the sporran and attach the fur, pressing it into place with a cocktail stick without flattening it.

5 Attach the silver clasp to the top of the sporran.

6 To make tassels, roll out the white Mexican paste very thinly. Cut out three 1cm (³⁄₈in) squares. Use the cutting wheel to make lots of cuts, leaving the top bands uncut. Roll up the tassels along the uncut bands. Dampen the backs of the tassels and attach them to the sporran.

7 Use piping gel to attach silver sugar balls to the top of each tassel and at the top of the silver clasp.

Acknowledgements
My thanks to all at Search Press and to
Paul Bricknell for the photography

You are invited to visit the
author's website:
www.franklysweet.co.uk
for more information and
video tutorials.

Publisher's Note
If you would like more information
about sugarcraft, try the following
books by the same author, all
published by Search Press:
Twenty to Make Sugar Animals
Twenty to Make Sugar Birds
Twenty to Make Sugar Fairies
Sensational Sugar Animals
Mini Sugar Shoes